# Pawsitive Connection

*Heartwarming stories of animals finding
people when we need them most*

## Volume I

*Stacey Ritz*

Copyright © 2014 Rockville Publishing

All rights reserved

ISBN-10: 1502778327

*To the animals.*
*Big or small, weak or strong, loved or homeless-all*
*are deserving of kindness and compassion.*

# Acknowledgments

A special thank you to my friends and family for your unwavering support in my unconventional life endeavors; I am so grateful for your listening ears and your open hearts. From my earliest memories I dreamed of being an author and I began sharing stories with anyone who would listen from the moment I learned to talk. My love of animals is innate; I feel blessed to come from a long line of big-hearted individuals who are in-tune with doing what's best for other living beings and the planet.

I am grateful to have co-founded Advocates 4 Animals, Inc. with my best friend in the entire world, my partner who is there for me through thick and thin, the one who doesn't just stand beside me as I live my dream, but jumps right in and experiences it all with me. I can't imagine life without you!

Thank you to everyone who has and continues to support Advocates 4 Animals plethora of life-saving programs; our committed adopters, our regular donors, those who sponsor special needs pets, our volunteers and of course the backbone of our organization- the foster families. It is because of each of you that miracles continue to happen each and every day. Lives that would otherwise perish under unspeakable circumstances instead have the ability to thrive because of your devotion and care. So often people tell me they "cannot do much to help, but can offer only a little." Whether it is a donation (item or financial), your kind words or any positive action on behalf of animals in need- we need it all. No action is too small to make a difference and it truly takes us all working together to continue making an impact on lives in need. Never underestimate the power of a positive action and never underestimate the power of yourself. When we all work together towards the common goal of greater good, amazing things happen and I feel so lucky to be witness to this again and again.

I am so appreciative for everyone who has shared and trusted me with their personal stories of the human-animal bond; thank you for inviting me into your lives and thank you for helping animals in need. The world is a better place because of you.

Last but certainly not least, a warm thank you to the pets themselves. Thank you for finding so many of us (humans) when we are most in need, even in the times when we don't know it yet (which so often is the case). Thank you for trusting us despite the horrors and difficulties you may have previously endured. Thank you for teaching us so many lessons about what is truly important in life, and thank you for letting us be a part of yours. It is my deepest wish that one day the entire human race will embrace kindness and respect towards all living beings. For now, I continue to promise to use my words, my stories and my actions to make a positive impact on as many lives as possible.

# Table of Contents

# Forward

We save each other. I am grateful to experience the power of positive connection time and again throughout my life. I started rescuing stray and injured animals in need as soon as I could walk, so I suppose it has always been in my DNA to co-found an animal welfare organization to assist animals in need on a larger platform. As for my words- my parents recorded my first word as *"talks a lot!"* in my neatly kept baby book. They claim that once I started talking, I didn't stop. I guess some things never change. I channel that raw spirit and energy into my writing, in an effort to share my experiences with you.

Life teaches us many lessons over the course of our years. If we are lucky, we learn that life isn't about money or things; life is about connection to other living beings. My experience continues to teach me that we often surround ourselves with mirror images of our inner selves. When we feel scared, we may witness that same phenomenon in others. When we are ready to move forward and heal from persisting deep wounds, we align ourselves with those who will support our transformation. When we're uncertain about the trajectory of our life, we see that same fear in those around us. So often it is our companion animals who find us when we are most in need. From my own ongoing adventures in animal rescue to the heartwarming stories that have been shared with me by others, I am absolutely certain that the human-animal bond has the power to heal, transform and enlighten each of our lives.

This book is a collection of true stories of *Pawsitive Connection* between pets (both cats and dogs) and humans, written from my own observations and opinions. It is my hope that the stories will resonate with each of you, as in the end, we are all connected. Animals have a mystical way of finding us when we need them most, even if we don't know it yet. But it is up to us to be alert and accepting of their healing powers; and when we are miracles truly can occur.

# Chapter 1: The Power of Connection

*"Blessed in the person who has earned the love of an old dog." –Sydney Jeanne Seward*

The first night of her passing, I desperately wished that I had a favorite toy or blanket to hold onto. We rescued her in 2011 after she had been callously dumped at a kill-shelter and deemed "vicious" (and therefore unadoptable). She was living in fear. Her feet had never known a ground other than rusty wire cages. She was heavily infested with fleas (to the point of having lost all of her fur). She had burn marks on her back end- guessed to be a type of torture method used in cruel breeding practices. The emaciated tan and white Chihuahua weighed just five pounds and her eyes were dim and hopeless. She wouldn't allow shelter volunteers near her- she would growl and lunge towards them, terrified for her life. Her nipples hung low from more than a decade of constant breeding. She was significantly underweight and dehydrated. Most of all, she was terrified.

I primarily fostered cats, but when the shelter volunteer reached out and sent me the photo of the elderly, terrified Chihuahua (who desperately needed rescue along with her suspected daughter, dumped at the shelter with her) my intuition told me I needed to save them, to foster them- to *give them a chance*. I was never a "small dog person" having shared my home in the past with large breed dogs such as Rottweiler mixes and the like. **But there is a**

**powerful force at play when you listen to your gut.**
And in this instance (I am so grateful) I listened to
mine.

*We named her Grandma*, as she was estimated to be
12-15 years old at the time of rescue. Her daughter
was estimated to be around five years old and after
she was given the medical care she needed, spayed
and fully vetted she was adopted to an incredibly
loving home where she was given the name Charlotte.

Grandma, on the other hand, had several serious
issues; life-threatening issues. Grandma's teeth were
each hanging by a thread- some of them hanging by
less than that. Her gums were filled with pus and she
was in significant pain.  She needed dental surgery
and all but three teeth removed immediately. She also
needed to be spayed. The day she was spayed, our
veterinarian called us to let us know if the spay had
taken place even one day later, Grandma would have
died. But we had the surgery done just in time. No
one knew, but when they opened Grandma up for her
spay surgery, it was discovered that she had
pyometra- which most likely was caused by being
bred in filthy conditions for more than a decade of
life. Grandma miraculously survived and made a full
recovery from her surgeries, all the while, we grew a
strong bond. She ran in the grass for the first time,
played with other dogs for the first time- and I mean
really played! She flipped her toys in the air and
growled with feistiness, as if she were a young puppy
just discovering life. Grandma, having lived her entire
life in a crate, was not potty trained. But she followed

the lead of my two resident dogs and caught on fairly quickly. Her eyes had a light that communicated her immense happiness to be alive and to be here.

Knowing her story, her age and her struggles with life-saving surgeries- and the strength of our bond that only continued to grow- we decided to officially adopt her (as if there were ever any question!). She fit like a glove. She got along great with our other two dogs and slept next to me in bed every night. She came to work with me, she went for car rides, we went on daily walks, lots of hikes in the woods and she had all of the spunk and energy of a young adult. Her hair grew in, and in time she reached a healthy, ideal weight of 9 lbs. Her burn marks went away and her happiness was palpable. She attached herself to me and I smiled and laughed more than I had in years.

In my personal life, I had suffered a debilitating sexual assault in 2008 and had been unable to cope with the ramifications surrounding the incident. I refused to speak about it and struggled to move forward. But when Grandma entered my life, things began to change. Grandma always wanted to be with me, sitting on my lap, snuggling, going for walks-you name it. She was right there by my side. And never in my life had I felt the loyalty of another living being in this strength. I had wonderful people in my life and I had shared my home with many special animals over the years, but there was something different about Grandma. Despite all that I had endured in my personal life, I knew Grandma would not abandon me emotionally. I knew I could just be me and I was accepted. There was something huge in that realization- and it was the start of my journey of emotional transformation.

**Everything in our lives, everything that surrounds us is a mirror of ourselves.** Realizing this now I am in awe at the gravity of its truth. And as for the Grandma and me, we healed each other.

We had three wonderful years. **I find myself wishing for one more day, one more walk, one more ride in the car…but I know that would only leave me wishing for another.** I miss her dearly and I feel lost without her. The month before she passed I began to feel a transformation in myself. I began to feel healed from the past trauma. I was able to let it go and move forward. I was living again. I was laughing again. My relationships had grown stronger and I had learned to trust- a gift I never expected would come.

Looking back, I realize the many lessons Grandma taught me- and continues to teach me even in her absence. She taught me that it's okay to be an adult and play- in fact it makes life so much more fun! She taught me that connection is real. She taught me that our eyes truly are the gateway to the soul. Grandma taught me that it's important to really listen when someone you love is talking to you, and she taught me that it's okay to look silly when you're excited. *The important thing is to be excited each and every time you see the ones you love-* never feel embarrassed to express your love- because you never know how many of those moments you'll have. She taught me that if you make known what you want in life (persistence!) that you will inevitably get it. She taught me to laugh. She taught me to never give up hope because you never know what might be around the next bend. She taught me that connection is what makes life worth living. She taught me to not be afraid of showing my teeth (it's okay to growl if something- or someone- bothers you); *speak up!* She taught me the meaning of unconditional love. And perhaps most of all, Grandma taught me to put the ones you connect with in life first. **If you have someone who loves you and you love them back you are incredibly lucky and blessed.**

As Grandma made a full recovery of her own and thrived, I began following her lead. Many times, talking about her in conversations served as an ice-breaker (given her unique name and her story). She went on beach vacations and even spent time in New York City with me walking through the hustle and bustle of it all. We were there for each other through our transformations.

Every day of her life, since rescue, was filled with happiness, laughter and love. During her final week she continued to have the same spunk she's carried with her since rescue; but at night she would insist on sleeping pressed tightly against me, her head on my pillow. My intuition told me her time was nearing and I tried my best to stay up for as long as I could each night giving her belly rubs and telling her how much I loved her. The day she passed, her breathing had quickly become strained. Her heart was giving out from old age. Her eyes told me she was ready for my help and we called our veterinarian. I held her in a blanket on my lap and before we left our street, from my lap and cradled in my arms, Grandma glanced up at me one last time and then quickly buried her head in the crook of my arm as I felt her leave. And just like that, she was gone.

Now I find myself wishing I had a favorite toy or blanket of hers to treasure. But then I was reminded that she didn't have a favorite of those things because I was her favorite thing. And what more could I ask for? *Knowing this was perhaps one of the greatest gifts she gave me.*

I believe that often animals find us at the right times. We may not recognize it in the moment, but something else is at play. Two days after Grandma's passing, still a wreck in her absence, I received a message to call my own Grandma (my human Grandma). It sounded urgent. I did my best to muster up the strength to talk through my own pain (and lots of tears) – and made the call to my Grandma. While not divulging the conversation in its totality, the talk we had that night was the most personal, meaningful conversation we had ever had. She told me that she (not knowing about Grandma's passing) had an overwhelming urge to speak with me this week. I was humbled by her words and a special promise she asked me to make to her during that phone call. Throughout the conversation she repeatedly thanked me for calling her and told me how happy it made her to feel near me. It's a feeling and a conversation I will never forget.

When I woke up the next morning the Native American saying, *"There are more things unseen and unknown than known and seen"* played on repeat in my head.

As published in Advocates 4 Animals Blog – August 2014

# A Few of the things Grandma taught me:

- It's okay to be goofy with the ones you love. Who cares what you look like? Happiness and laughter are what life is all about!

- It doesn't matter how old or young you are- when you have the opportunity to run through the grass with your bare feet, do it with wild abandonment.

- Never stop being curious. Adventure can always be found when your eyes are open.

- It's okay to growl when you're upset. It's healthy to show your true emotions.

- When you see someone you love, show your excitement (don't hold back)!

- It's okay to ask for help. When you're too tired to keep going, ask for help and it will come.

- Don't hide yourself away. Be proud of who you are. When you are your authentic self you will undoubtedly make others smile.

- Always sleep in the position that is most comfortable. No questions asked.

- It's okay to bury your head under the covers when you don't want to get up in the morning. Sometimes a few more minutes of quiet can go a long way.

- Barking is good! If something doesn't seem right, speak up.

- Enjoy the sunshine. Get outside daily and bask in the light- you'll be glad you did.

- Never underestimate the power of love and loyalty.

An additional story, *"Grandma's Journey"* has been published in Chicken Soup for the Soul: *The Dog Did What?* –2014

# Chapter 2: Love Comes in Many Forms

*"Any glimpse into the life of an animal quickens our own and makes it so much the larger and better in every way." –John Muir*

With a handful of grown children of her own, twenty plus grandchildren and a few sprinkles of great grandchildren, Sophie couldn't have felt more proud. At ninety-four years of age, Sophie felt blessed to have been married over seventy years. Being active and social in her community on a daily basis, she and her husband continued to live independently in their quiet Ohio Cape Cod home. Having maintained strong health, Sophie and her family had no way of knowing that a day of shopping would bring about a significant and sudden life change.

Just as they had done every day for nearly five years, two furry black tails strolled side by side throughout the long and narrow corridor of the Cincinnati nursing home. Walking gracefully in and out of room after room, the two felines volunteered their time and efforts visiting with residents in return for being given a safe, loving home, plenty of great food and unlimited attention.

What could be better?

The feline duo comforted anyone who requested their assistance (and also those who did not).

Sophie was a new resident at the nursing home and was oblivious to the feline duo. After suffering a heart-attack while enjoying an evening of shopping and dinner with friends and family, Sophie found herself in what felt like a small college dorm room, with a new roommate included. She was frustrated that she could not return home to be with her husband. She longed to be in the comfort of her own home with the familiar surroundings that had embraced her life for years. Feeling lonely, confused and desperate to leave the facility which she determined was only

for those who were counting down their last moments of life, Sophie demanded the nurses release her and allow her to drive home.

In no condition to drive, Sophie felt restless from her own frustrations and beyond exhausted from her medical ailments. The small bedroom window transformed from black midnight skies giving way to bursting rays of sun. A new day was starting. The nurse thrust back the heavy

beige curtains as Sophie strained to adjust her eyes to the daylight. Her hand felt soft and a mild vibration seemed to pulsate through her fingers.

It must be the millions of medications, Sophie thought angrily to herself.

Letting out a small chuckle, the nurse neared Sophie's bedside. "Looks like the feline duo found a new friend." She glanced down towards Sophie's right hand. There sat the two sleek black felines, curled up side by side in Sophie's bed. One had positioned herself just under her fingers, the other pressed right up alongside her stomach. Both cats were relaxed, not seeming to have a care in the world.

"Well...I....Where did...?" Sophie stumbled on her words. "I...I must be dreaming. I'm not a fan of cats. You can take them away." She ordered.

The days marched on and Sophie began to find herself spending more and more time with the so called feline duo. Most mornings she would wake up with one or both cats by her side. During the day she would receive several unsolicited visits from both felines. Sophie petted them, talked to them and listened closely to their soft purrs. She closely studied the slight tiger stripes in their dark black fur that could only been seen in the brightest rays of sunlight. She found herself beginning to wonder about their personal stories.

How did they end up at the shelter?

Did they have names?

Her roommate had previously suffered from a stroke and was unable to speak. No one was around to answer Sophie's newly formed questions. The nurses were always in and out and onto the next patient; they seemed to lack the time to respond to her cat questions.

Oh well.

Sophie let out a sigh. I will just call you Cleo, and you I will call Billy. Yep, Cleo and Billy. *Purr-fect!* She smiled to herself. A smile was something that had eluded Sophie since her entry into the nursing home nearly a week earlier.

The nurse smiled again, this time stroking one of the cats and then placing her hand gently on Sophie's forearm. "Miss Sophie, the cats live here. They like you." She paused. "I'm not going to take them away. They are just visiting with you, honey." She looked Sophie sharply in the eyes. "Do you have a cat at home?"

Sophie shook her head, still feeling confused. 'We used to have a dog....I've never....I've never had a cat before. I'm not a cat person." She snapped.

"Well, it looks like the cats like you Miss Sophie. They're pretty popular around here. They've been here for about five years now. They were rescued from the shelter and they have given nothing but love to everyone who comes here. Give them a chance, I promise they won't bother you." And with that, the nurse sharply hung her chart on the wall and exited.

When Sophie's family members came to visit they began to notice an enormous difference in her demeanor. She no longer seemed angry or bitter about wanting to get home. Sophie of course still longed to move back home with her husband, free from the nurses and the small shared room. However, she seemed relaxed and at peace with knowing that she would return home after a short rest at the nursing facility. She exhibited a new found confidence and seemed to have a twinkle in her eyes. Her family couldn't help but wonder what had caused this incredible transformation over the course of just one week. Their curiosity flooded Sophie with questions-Are you meeting a lot of new people? Do you like the food? Are the nurses treating you well? How is your roommate? Have the other family members been visiting often?

Meanwhile, Cleo and Billy strolled up and down the corridor visiting other residents and holding their tails high in the air as they walked quietly through the building that had become known as their home.

Do you need anything mom? Would you like me to bring you a few magazines from the grocery store? The questions continued. Sophie, all the while, listened patiently to her children and grandchildren's concerned voices, but thinking only about the feline duo. She wondered who they were visiting; she wondered when they would stop by her room to visit again that day.

"Could you get me a pack of kitty treats?" Sophie blurted.

Furrowed eyebrows swept the room full of concerned family members. Sophie could tell they all thought she was confused and unsure of what she was asking.

"Could you get a pack of cat treats at the grocery store and bring them to me?" She repeated with a smile.

"Mom, you don't have a cat."

Cleo and Billy, tails high and entwined, came trotting down the hall, making a beeline for Sophie. A tear came to Sophie's eye, but she was quick to wipe it away. A nurse walking by knew what Sophie was hoping for and softly handed her a fist full of cat treats. Sophie reached out her hand, this time handing the treats to her son and nodded towards the feline duo.

As he knelt on the ground to supply the much desired treats, Sophie watched with a twinkle in her eyes. "Thank you." She whispered quietly while watching the cats. "Thank you so much."

# Chapter 3: When Sally Met Harry

*"My little dog; a heartbeat at my feet."* –Edith
Wharton

He stumbled into their hearts when he found them at work. He trotted onto the grounds and day after day he came back, his little beady eyes pleading for food, water and attention. There weren't many houses around, just an old country road and though they searched, an owner never came forward. The little black and white dog was clearly older, although spry for what it appeared he had endured. His tail was docked, yet he hadn't been neutered. His body was frail and his hair loose from the attack of fleas. After several weeks of the little dog coming back each day for food and comfort, he quickly became accustomed to the touch of a gentle hand. He received unlimited love and affection from employees and a special fleece bed had been made just for the little guy.

The young employees who first encountered the small needy dog named him *Harry*. But soon the summer season was over and the workers retreated back to college, leaving Harry behind. But Harry was not alone; he had nuzzled his way into two hearts that were certain to keep him safe. That's when *Sally Met Harry*, officially. Harry was welcomed into the home of Sally and her husband, while still traveling each day to and from their house to their place of work; the same place where he first had been rescued. Harry received unlimited love and attention, lots of cuddle time and he rode everywhere in the car with them.

Harry became quickly attached to Sally, riding next to her in the car, sleeping curled up next to her at night and trotting after her with the spunk of a young pup. The two were inseparable and although Sally didn't notice at the time, Harry's timing couldn't have been more fitting. Harry found Sally at a time when she needed him most. Having raised her children and watched the first two leave the nest, her third was at the age of preparing to follow suit. Sally found herself missing the days of driving her children to sports practices and attending their concerts. It was hard enough when their first child left for college, but now that her youngest was preparing for flight, Sally found herself longing to nurture and care for another. Harry arrived at exactly the right time.

Harry loved both Sally and her husband, but it was clear to everyone who met them that he had a special attachment to Sally. He followed at her feet wherever she went. When they watched television in the evenings he was always curled up in her lap, without a care in the world. When they went for long walks, Harry accompanied them staying ever steady at her side. When they prepared for the next wedding, Harry came along to help with the festivities too. Harry traveled by Sally's side during the excitement of meeting the couple's first grandchild. Harry was there for the hard times too. He never left Sally's side as she ached over the sudden health scare that hit her own father. He stood by her through the tears and the laughter as a faithful friend always does, never placing judgment but simply offering a soft place to land.

Continuing to travel to and from work with his guardians, Harry became a staple at the place of business. Customers asked about Harry and wondered how he was doing in his senior years. Harry stuck by Sally's side and when she was busy with work he tended to keep to himself. But never the less, visiting customers latched on to Harry and his story of rescue and loved seeing him trot around beside Sally's feet, his dark brown eyes staring up at her, eager to be held.

As the years plodded on, Harry lost much of his hearing and sight. A large cancerous tumor began growing and veterinarians confirmed that his age made the risk of surgery too risky. Most of his teeth had fallen out and his tongue hung to one side, adding to his unique look. One ear now flopped forward as the other stood tall. His stark black and white fur now filled in with increasing specks of gray. Harry's age was showing, he began sleeping longer and taking more naps. He had days full of vitality and others that showed signs of his growing aches and pains. But through it all his loyalty never wavered as he aged with grace and dignity.

Shortly after the birth of their first grandchild, Harry began to fade. While at work one day (the same place where he had found his way to their hearts so many years ago), Harry was resting comfortably at Sally's side, and Sally and her husband knew it was time. Sally scooped Harry up into her arms and cradled him as the tears began to flow. They made an appointment with the local veterinarian, not wanting Harry to suffer in his final moments. As they drove to the veterinarians office words were hard to find. Harry lay peacefully in Sally's arms looking back at her, thanking her for all that she had done. It had been eight glorious years and he was grateful for every one of them. As they pulled into the parking lot and found themselves walking towards the door, Sally continued cradling Harry in her arms as they each whispered their good-bye's, feeling the sting of tears rush down their cheeks. They hoped they were doing the right thing, they hoped Harry knew they just wanted him to pass peacefully. They hoped he knew how much they loved him and how they would never forget him. They hoped…and as they opened the door to the veterinary office, Sally placed her foot on the threshold of the doorway and at that very moment she felt Harry pass. His little heart stopped beating and he lay peacefully in her arms. The couple felt it was Harry's way of leaving on his own terms- in the comfort of their arms. It was as if Harry knew that it was okay to go; he knew Sally would be okay now. And that's exactly when he left.

Harry entered Sally's life when she faced the daunting transition of an empty nest. He didn't leave her side until the birth of her first grandchild occurred and somehow he must have known that she had a little one to help care for again; although I have a hunch that Harry will always remain with Sally in spirit. The couple's second grandchild was born just seven months after Harry's passing. Sally still misses Harry's presence and at times she finds herself thinking he'll still be trotting beside her feet, she knows without question that he will always be with her in her heart and in so many memories. He wiggled his way into her heart all those years ago when he first arrived, tattered and torn and there he will remain loyal forever, an angel who came in disguise.

# Chapter 4: Allowing the Past to Fuel the Future

*"Our perfect companions never have fewer than four feet." -Colette*

Her screams were violent and full of fury. Scurrying around her tiny apartment, hands raised in the air and her mouth full of obscenities, the woman ran back and forth with wild abandon. The two adult cats out sprinted her with each new chase. Clearly terrified for their lives, the cat's state of panic only continued to grow. Feeling helpless as I stood near the door, I tried to interrupt the chaos before me, but it was no use. I was merely a fly on the wall. That cat's weren't calming down and the woman's rampage marched on.

We had been contacted by the guardian of two unaltered Bengal cats in need of assistance. The woman claimed to be moving and added with an air of distain, *"They are nasty cats anyway. Just nasty."* I was available to foster two new cats at that time as part of Advocates 4 Animals rescue/adoption program, yet I had no way of knowing all that was about to come my way. The woman signed over her cats as she scrunched her nose and rolled her eyes. When I turned to leave instead of saying good-bye she wiped her hands together and closed the door before my heals were across the threshold. The two cats were in a scuffle inside of the carrier and I was anxious to reach the car.

Our veterinarians and staff were unable to hold the cats as they growled and scratched, desperate for revenge from their prior life. I took them home, feeling a bit bewildered at the new project I had just embarked on. The performance of their former guardian replayed through my mind, as did her words. It hadn't registered amongst the chaos, but her words sifted into my brain as I sat watching the two girls in their crate, wondering what to do with two untouchable cats. She had told me she shipped them around the world to be bred. Over and over again the cats were "mailed" from one location to another to be impregnated by another Bengal cat, have babies and watch their babies be taken and sold for greedy profits.

I sat watching the two cats growling at each other and at me from behind the bars of their large crate. My heart felt heavy as I realized all that they had endured. Never had they known a kind hand. Never had they experienced the power of a loving bond with any other living being. They had been used again and again for someone else's personal gain.

Slowly, I reached to open the crate door. I spoke softly and kept my energy in check. I petted one cat on the top of her head as the other watched carefully from the back of the crate. Their terrified bodies were stone and their eyes were solid steel. Their past environment had created their current demeanor – survival mode. A moment later the hissing began and the two cats started bouncing around the crate like jumping beans. I closed the door, feeling my heart race. I refused to believe they were "nasty cats"; but I knew they were petrified. I could hardly imagine the horrors they had endured, how were they to know that the nightmare was over?

First things first, the cats needed names; Polly and Portia. Next, I needed to create a stable, calm environment for the cats. I gave them the small extra bedroom in the house, setting up plush pet beds, two litter-boxes and several food and water bowls with a buffet of nutritious options for their pallet. I plugged in a small radio and adjusted the volume to low as I moved the dial to a soft rock station. I rearranged the room so that the cats could sit on the bed to look out the window when they were ready. Once the room was set and their names were announced I sat beside the crate again, slowly opening the door. They crept out from the crate one at a time, slithering across the floor like snakes. They made a quick stop to smell the food and then vanished under the safety of the bed-skirt. It was going to take time; a lot of time. But I was in it for the long haul. With a calm environment, the stability of regular food, water and routine- and with given names, Polly and Portia would come around in their own time. There was no need to rush what would take care of itself.

The first month of extensive rehabilitation, Polly and Portia hid under the bed refusing to be seen. I read aloud and spoke to them so that they could become familiar with my voice. They weren't growling or hissing, just understandably scared after the past they had endured. The following month they began to emerge and my heart soared. Slowly, they crept towards me, hesitant but curious. With a little more time, their tails raised high into the air showing a sense of confidence. I sat on the floor and let them come towards me; I didn't want to startle them and I wanted the progress to be on their own terms so that it would last. Most of all, I wanted them to learn that there are kind humans and from this point forward they would always be in caring hands. It was a rocky road; some days were better than others but what mattered was that progress was being made. Once Polly and Portia began to regularly trot up to me as I entered their room (even before I could sit down) and once they comfortably sat in my lap, I knew I could breathe a sigh of relief; they were on their way!

After nearly six-months of strenuous rehabilitation work, Polly and Portia made great strides. They had successfully completed their veterinary health checks, they were spayed, vaccinated and fully vetted and the two cats were comfortable in their space. While they each understandably preferred being an only cat, the two tolerated each other while working through the rehabilitation process. Within a few additional months, Polly and Portia were ready to begin meeting potential adopters although we knew placing them in the appropriate home was key to their future happiness and well-being.

Polly was adopted as an only cat to a special needs adult who longed for a companion to keep her company during her quiet days at home. Polly was the perfect fit! The moment she met her adopter she hopped in her lap and then onto her bed. It has been five years since the adoption and we still receive wonderful updates from Polly's adopter about the wonderful life the two lead together.

Portia was the more reserved of the two felines, but still had become very friendly to those she trusted. After receiving what seemed to be the ideal adoption application for this very special feline, we took Portia to meet her potential adopter in his home with a warning that Portia would most likely hide and be incredibly reclusive during the first meet and greet session. But much to our surprise, as we all sat on the living room floor and waited for Portia to poke her head out from behind her pet carrier door, Portia slowly placed her paws on the carpet and trotted over to meet her adopter. She placed herself next to him, her eyes full of content as my eyes filled with happy tears. It had taken nearly a year for her to achieve a sense of peace and relaxation and now here she was sprawled out beside her adopter as if she didn't have a care in the world. Animals never cease to amaze me and the power of forgiveness towards the human-race that Portia demonstrated in that moment rendered me speechless.

The adoption was a success not only in knowing that Portia found a well-matched forever home, but in learning that Portia had later completed training to become a certified therapy cat and was now helping countless others find happiness in their darkest moments. Portia's adopter himself had faced unspeakable childhood abuse and from that the two forged an everlasting bond that carried them forward into a remarkable future. Instead of allowing their pasts to define them, the unlikely pair used their past and their newly formed bond to change the trajectory of their lives for the better.

# Chapter 5: With Paws and Poise

*"A meow massages the heart." –Stuart McMillan*

It is universally the most difficult time in our lives; when we lose a loved one. Standing in the funeral home making arrangements while grieving such an enormous loss we can find ourselves feeling hopeless and lost. A cheery image never comes to mind when you hear the phrase "funeral home." But in Greenwood, Indiana G.H. Herrmann Funeral Home is doing what they can to help ease the process. In March of 2014 Ryan Trares of the Washington Times (AP)* reported the story of four special therapy dogs working at the aforementioned funeral home and yielding positive results. Jax, a "laid back Labrador" and three other certified therapy dogs work at the funeral home to provide comfort for those dealing with the death of a loved one. While Jax is said to be normally found "lounging around", Trares' article explains "...*when a grieving family walks through the door, his demeanor changes completely. Instinctively, he approaches slowly, offering companionship and a furry head to pet.*"

There are other funeral homes throughout the country also working with certified therapy dogs to help humans in a multitude of ways. Certified therapy dogs can be found in schools, hospitals, nursing homes and hospice centers.

So what about therapy cats? Yes, there is such a thing! Therapy cats work the same as therapy dogs, they help people in ways that no one else can. There are Reading Buddy programs across the nation that bring certified therapy cats (and dogs) to work with young children on their reading skills. Children can sit in a quiet area and practice reading aloud to the visiting therapy cat, therefore enhancing the child's confidence, reading skills and let's not forget, their overall happiness of course!

Studies show that pets help keep your blood pressure in check. *Pets.WebMD.com* reports that cats and dogs are good for your heart. And no, not just in the "my heart is pounding with cuteness overload" sort of way. Sharing your life and home with a pet is actually healthy for your heart. "Research has shown the long-term benefits of owning a cat include protection for your heart. Over the 20 years of one study, people who never owned a cat were 40% more likely to die of a heart attack than those who had. Another study showed that dog owners had a significantly better survival rate one year after a heart attack." *Pets.WebMD.com* goes on to discuss the topic of fewer strokes among cat owners. "Researchers aren't sure why. But cat owners have fewer strokes than people who don't own cats. It's partly due to the effects owning a pet can have on a person's circulation. But researchers speculate that cats may have a more calming effect on their owners than other animals do."

Here's a "Did you know?" that might surprise you (or maybe not!) Pets are natural mood enhancers. *Pets.WebMD.com* explains, "It only takes a few minutes with a dog or cat or watching fish swim to feel less anxious and less stressed. Your body actually goes through physical changes in that time that make a difference in your mood. The level of cortisol, a hormone associated with stress, is lowered. And the production of serotonin, a chemical associated with well-being, is increased."

Sharing your life with a pet also helps fight depression. Pets can keep you in better physical shape too! Playing with your pets, taking your dog for a walk, run or hike can all provide health benefits while having fun. Speaking of living a healthy life, children who grow up on a farm or in a home with a dog or cat are "less likely to develop allergies."

There is no end to the amazing benefits that pets provide. Dogs can sniff out cancer, cats and dogs can help those with diabetes and "seizure dogs" are trained to help people with epilepsy. There are search and rescue dogs who help save the lives of the missing, police dogs that help keep our communities safe and therapy cats who lend a listening ear.

Pets don't have to be "certified" to make a difference. In fact, our household pets are making an impact on our lives each and every day. How do your pets help you? It's not the training that we- *humans*- provide to pets that enable the pets to suddenly have these amazing talents and skills; it's the fact that **we continue to learn how to effectively communicate with the pets so that we can successfully learn the helpful and informative (often life-saving) information they already know.**

Perhaps the most astonishing trait of companion animals is that they remain forever committed to us, their faithful guardians. When times get tough, they don't disappear- *they show up*. When we need a shoulder to cry on, they are there. When we need to sing out loud and show our joy (and not be embarrassed) we know they won't judge us; instead they join in on the celebration. Pets are our loyal companions to the very end. It is impossible to count the ways in which they enhance our lives, but for each of us who share our hearts with a pet, we know that what really counts is our loyalty to one another; the promise of knowing that we'll be there, together through life's journey.

# Chapter 6: Floppy Ears and Unwavering Faith

*"An animal's eyes have the power to speak a great language." –Martin Buber*

He fit in the palm of one hand, floppy ears and all. We saved the little brown and black puppy from death row at a local shelter. Before we arrived to save the little guy, we hadn't even seen a photo. We were told there was a young dog in need of help that day. We didn't have a foster dog at the time and I was happy we were able to help. On the drive back from his rescue we stopped to visit my parents as they were finishing up a day of work. The moment I opened the car door I thought I saw a light flicker in their eyes. We named him Riley and as I watched the little brown-eyed puppy bounce around the grass and begin playing with my parent's senior dog. I spoke without further thought. "You should adopt him! He would fit right in. You could take him to work with you each day and the two dogs would enjoy each other's company." I pleaded knowing instinctively that it was the right fit. Although little Riley had only been with us a single day, my heart told me that he was exactly where he belonged as I watched my parents take turns holding him in their laps, their eyes sparkling with delight. Sure, they tried their best to act disinterested, but all of the signs were there. Riley was meant for them. He licked their faces and begged for their attention and that's exactly what he got that evening as we sat outside and marveled over the boundless energy of puppies.

As we fostered Riley I took him on frequent visits to see my parents on the weekends and after they had a chance to talk it over, they agreed that Riley was meant for them (well, I don't know if that's exactly how they saw it at the time; but it's how I perceived the situation). My parents loved him and wanted to adopt him, however they had three more months of the "busy season" at their business and wanted to wait to officially adopt him after that period. Oh and they added the stipulation that they would adopt him after he was successfully potty-trained. I had my work cut out for me. With two dogs of my own to help guide him, I hoped that potty-training little Riley would go smoothly. My parents also needed Riley to be a good "rider"-meaning that he needed to do well riding in the car. I promised that he would meet their wishes and I would train him over the upcoming months.

Car ride after car ride Riley's stomach would become upset and he would shower me with warm goop. I'll spare you any further details. He insisted on riding on my lap (so did my small dog), so together the two of them squeezed in and held their ground as I focused on the road. But it was inevitable, each trip Riley would "toss his cookies"- *on me*- and each trip I vowed to keep trying. I knew it was just a matter of the little guy getting used to car trips. Persistence is always the key when you're working towards a worthy goal.

The little guy was so darn cute that I made the mistake of giving into his cries and letting him snuggle up in bed at night. I'm sure you can guess what happened there. He showered me in warm puppy urine. I wasn't upset, it was my decision that caused the mishap, but what I'm trying to convey is that it was a long journey to training the adorable floppy eared puppy. But it was more than worth it, it always is.

After three-months of training, Riley grew and was neutered and fully vetted. He was potty-trained and loved going for car rides. No more "tossing his cookies". Although he was growing, he still insisted on sitting on top of my lap while in the car, something he still does today with his forever guardians (adopters). My parents officially adopted Riley and he fit like a glove. He rode to and from work with them each day and followed their senior dog around like an obedient protégé. The two rescue dogs spent time snuggling up together on their dog beds and enjoying their nutritious dinners side by side each night, their tails wagging simultaneously in the air. Riley was as easy going as a dog could be. His short little legs and big brown eyes bustled through the many customers and he quickly made friends with all ages and kinds of other life forms. Riley became a favorite of visitors to my parents business and he often poses for photos with school groups. He is much like a movie-star (in his own right)!

As Riley quickly settled into his forever home, although he was bonded with both of his guardians and his senior canine brother, he grew especially fond of my dad. He slept by his side, he trotted along next to his feet on any excursion my dad took pursuit in. Riley rides on my dad's lap every single car ride; not one has been missed. He goes to work with him each day and on the occasion that Riley stays at home with my mom, waiting on my dad to come back from running an errand, he watches faithfully by the front door waiting for his best friend to return. The pure magic that exists between the two is obvious. Once, while my dad waded out into a brisk river to help cut a large tree blocking the way, Riley jumped in trying to save him. Riley's not fond of swimming but his mentality with my dad has always been "you jump, I jump."

Following the adoption of Riley, my dad's own dad began battling health issues. Having been especially close with his dad, this began a very difficult time in his life. Throughout the troubling times Riley remained close by my dad's side. He came with my parents to visit and shower my grandpa with endless love. Riley always knew just how to bring a smile to anyone's face. When my grandpa passed away, Riley was there to aid my dad – my parents – in their grieving. As the faithful companion that he is, Riley stayed true to his unwavering loyalty. Although grown into his adult body now, Riley's floppy ears and big brown eyes brought comfort to his guardians during a time of great need. Although no one could bring back my grandpa, Riley provided his assistance through the gift of love. The pain of losing a family member, a loved one who gave life to us, who raised us and who taught us so much of what we know, is something that never goes away. The sting of loss remains, even with the passage of time. The saying goes "time heals all wounds" and maybe that is true, but when you survive the loss of a loved one, life is forever changed. Whether Riley understands this or not, we may never know. But one thing we all know for sure is that Riley recognizes energy and he is committed to living each breath to its fullest.

When I recently lost my own dog to old age I was devastated. The vulnerability of loss that I shared through conversations with my parents seemed to bring us closer together. I guess that's what vulnerability does, when we stop being afraid of what other people might think, when we show our true colors and expose our wounds, that's when we see ourselves in others- that's when we connect. In one way or another we have all experienced the loss of a loved one- whether through a relationship breaking up or through death. Loss is universal and if we're brave enough to share that loss we can help each other heal. I stood with my dad while visiting one evening and we watched in the distance as Riley greeted the customers of their business and seemed to be beaming from ear to ear. "I wish I just had one more day with him…" My dad recounted in reference to his own dad. But the reality is we never know how many days we have. The unpredictability of the future is as certain as anything on the planet. Vulnerability may connect us- and possibly even more so during times of great loss- but the not knowing connects us too because it's universal. Every living being from the smallest insect to the elephant knows that each day holds no promises. We don't know how long we have.

As we stood in silence watching Riley romp around in the grass and make friends in every direction he looked, I think we both understood the notion that life is a gift, not to be wasted. The deep wounds of loss can leave us aching to rewind time, but the hour-glass keeps on sifting and time marches on.

While there are no certainties in life, there is the ability to choose our actions and our words. We can decide to be vulnerable with others and risk making a meaningful connection or we can hide away burying ourselves in despair. The point is that we don't get to decide how long we have but we do get to decide how we use the time that we are given. Riley uses his time to make an unlimited amount of friends and bask in the limelight while all the while staying undeniably true to his loyal guardians. I don't think Riley ever set out to prepare himself to help my dad with such an enormous transition in his adult life, but because he knows home is wherever my dad is, he's up for anything that comes their way. That's how I strive to live my life as I continue to grow…to be open to the ever changing twists and turns that life will surely bring and to learn to smile along the way.

# Chapter 7: Purr-fect Match

*"Lots of people talk to animals…Not very many listen, though…That's the problem."*
*–Benjamin Hoff*

Black felines statistically take longer to find homes than any other breed (or "look") or cats. Some muse that this may be from the fact that the human eye is drawn to light colors. Others blame it on the inability for black cats to "stand out" in photographs while some place the aversion on [the myth of] black cats being bad luck. Regardless of the reason, black cats need loving homes too!

When a little solid black kitten named Farrah was rescued from death row at the local animal shelter (meaning she was next on the list to be "euthanized for space") she had no idea what was in store for her. As space allows, Advocates 4 Animals rescue/adoption program works with some of the more forward thinking county shelters/pounds to save lives on death row. It is our hope that one day through continued collaboration with approved 501(c)3 animal welfare organizations shelters and pounds across the country will embrace the No Kill Movement with open arms. But at the present time we are still fighting an up-hill battle. The nation as a whole kills more than 50% of healthy, adoptable shelter pets. Cats are the number one breed/pet killed by shelter euthanasia, followed by Chihuahua's and then Pit-Bull Terriers. **Shelter euthanasia is also the number one cause of death in cats, more than any**

**disease.** We have been inundated with stories from former shelter/pound workers who tell us the horrors of being assigned the job of choosing which pets die each new day and often it is the black cats who go first.

When we work collaboratively with shelters who want to save lives (and in turn, save their municipalities funds) we can make a difference in lives that are begging for our assistance. The way it typically works is you must go through a separate process with each shelter to demonstrate your credentials (i.e. 501(c)3 status, proven adoption numbers, etc.) and then communicate with the shelter on a regular basis to learn about the animals they will not place up for adoption (for a variety of reasons ranging from shy, scared, sick, special needs, senior status, etc.) and when there is a pet(s) that your organization is able and willing to save (AKA pull to safety) you pay a pull fee for each pet (generally they have no vetting to speak of); therefore you are paying the shelter a fee to take an animal they otherwise would have spent money on to needlessly euthanize. It's a win-win situation for the animals, for the tax-payers, for the shelter facility and for the future adopters of these special pets.

But I digress. Saving animals on death row from shelters/pounds is no small feat. When egos can be thrown aside and we all work together towards saving lives, amazing triumphs can be accomplished. It's not about which organization saved the animal- or how many animals' one particular group saves- it's about SAVING them. *Every life matters.*

Farrah, the little black kitten was saved amongst a bundle of other needy kittens. Each one entered our rescue/adoption program and received full vetting prior to entering their volunteer foster homes. Farrah and the other rescued kittens thrived under the loving touch of their temporary homes. But Farrah watched as each kitten in the group became adopted by loving, committed families. She was continuously overlooked, not for lack of personality, but simply for her "standard look." She bounced around and played, she cuddled up in laps and she batted her big green eyes towards every potential adopter who came to visit.

After all of the other kittens had been adopted, Farrah was growing quickly and becoming accustomed to the daily routine of her foster home. But after a bit more time the forever home she could once only dream of found her with open arms.

When we took Farrah to meet her potential adopters, they explained to us how adopting Farrah (who was putting on quite the show flipping toys in the air and snuggling up against the young girl) was incredibly meaningful to them as a family. The couples youngest daughter had been recently adopted herself. With the two older children in the family being biological children, Casey (their newly adopted six-year old daughter) had not been born in the United States. The family sported blond curly hair while Casey's hair was straight and shiny black. Casey had been having a difficult time with the transition to her adopted home and her parents wanted to help. During her first few months with her adopted family, young Casey had asked for a friend that had the same color of hair as hers. Remembering her words and taking them to heart, her parents combined Casey's love for animals and her need for assistance during this major transition in her life. The family wanted to adopt Farrah the black furred kitten, as a special friend for their daughter Casey. "Farrah became someone for [Casey] to talk to when she felt she had nowhere to turn. Farrah followed her around the house like a puppy from day one." The first thing Casey said when she met Farrah (and Farrah quickly curled up in her lap with a roaring purr) was, "Her hair looks just like mine!" She was beaming with a smile that stretched from ear to ear.

Farrah helped Casey realize that she was exactly where she needed to be; she belonged in her home, surrounded by endless love. And Casey continues to provide endless love to Farrah as they continue to age together. In a world where the only certainty is change, Farrah and Casey know that no matter what they will always stand by each other's side. Through the twists and turns of life, through both the sad and happy times, the girls will keep one another company, their matching beautiful shiny black hair glistening in the sunlight of another promising day. Together this bonded pair know without a shadow of a doubt that they are connected; they may not know the exact details of each other's beginnings, but they know all they need to, to understand that love and connection are the foundations for a life well-lived.

# Chapter 8: Lessons of Love

*"When you open your heart to a pet, your world can only change for the better." –Stacey Ritz*

The music was blaring, it ran through her fingers and toes as they moved from one beat to the next. Without a care in the world, the high school senior felt that anything was possible as she drove down the busy freeway. Ashley's world was about to change without warning; as she reached forward to adjust the volume the corner of her eye caught a glimpse of fluff. Her fingers stopped tapping, her toes instinctively moved towards the brakes; all the while the music blared, echoing off the windows as Ashley's heart felt ripped from her chest.

The little gray ball of fluff was a kitten screaming for her life, stuck on the narrow cement divide between endless lanes of hectic traffic. It never occurred to Ashley that she shouldn't help. It never crossed her mind that she ought to phone professionals to assist her. Ashley's instincts took over as she placed the car's blinker lights on and found a stretch of cement to pull over among the passing traffic. Cars honked, others drove on by, but Ashley stayed focused. "It's crazy to think back to that moment now" Ashley recounted, "I never thought about the possibility of the kitten running out into traffic…that could have easily happened. There were multiple lanes of traffic on each side of the two-foot tall cement divide where the little ball of fluff sat, screaming anxiously for help. But I am so grateful for my instincts." Having pulled off to the side of the freeway, Ashley's blinkers remained on and she left several feet between the edge of her car before the traffic lanes began. Slowly, she backed her car towards the needy kitten, the windows both rolled down on her passenger side. As she reached the meowing fluff ball she called to her, begging her to jump inside. "I couldn't believe it." Ashley shared. Astonishingly the kitten jumped through the open window and climbed straight towards Ashley's lap, shaking in nervous terror.

Having never shared her life (or home) with an animal previously, Ashley's world instantly changed, as did the fluff balls. No one knows how the little kitten ended up in the position she did, but the outcome tells the real story. Ashley named her rescued kitten Squirt. She hand fed her as she helped her gain much needed strength and weight. Squirt was covered in fleas and dirt and needed veterinary care; Ashley saw to it that the extra money from her part-time job outside of school went to provide for her new friend. When Ashley moved out of the house after graduation, Squirt of course came with her too. Squirt remained in her life as Ashley figured out her own trajectory while passing through the obstacles of various careers, boyfriends and other life challenges. Through it all, Squirt remained by her side.

It was because of Ashley's original encounter with Squirt that she became inspired to give back to other animals. She realized that she couldn't save every animal in need, but that there were small actions she could take to make a difference. Ashley began using the money she had left over (after paying her bills) to purchase pet food and toys to donate to the local animal shelter. Inevitably Ashley encountered other cats in need and learned about the No Kill Movement which encompasses privately operated animal rescue and welfare organizations. She worked together with local advocates and volunteers to provide full vetting and volunteer foster homes within the rescue networks until adopters could be found for each cat in need. Each time she helped a cat and forged a connection with a local animal rescue organization, Ashley's invested interest in local efforts to save animals in need continued to grow. Today, Ashley and her husband work together to donate funds and items to local No Kill organizations that are truly making a difference in their community.

Prior to her encounter with Squirt, Ashley described herself as "…in my own world. I wasn't aware of the struggles and needs of others until I saw Squirt meowing for help. He was in such a hopeless situation, yet he was able to be saved. It's a moment I will never forget." A moment of impact changed Ashley's perceptions on life and on giving back; though just a teen at the time, Ashley's life became forever changed when she experienced the power of lending a helping hand. *She* never expected to be changed; in fact, she never expected anything. The day Ashley pulled off to the side of the road to help a frightened life in need, she was simply following her instincts and because of her heroic actions she learned the value of self-less compassion. Since the day Ashley saved Squirt, many additional lives have been touched and/or saved because of her kindness. Ashley realizes that even small actions can make enormous impacts and to this day she continues following her heart which she shares, "It's all thanks to Squirt."

# Chapter 9: At Your Service!

*"A kitten is the rosebud in the garden of the animal kingdom." –Robert Southey*

It was a heart aneurism. Being in his eighties, doctors weren't sure if he would recover from such a horrendous ordeal. Alice, his wife of more than sixty-years was understandably overwhelmed at the sudden turn of events. The married couple lived a quiet life together on their farm, generally sharing their property and home with a beloved dog. The old farm buildings on the land lay dormant of animals. The peaceful sounds of chirping crickets and buzzing cicadas filled the evening air as they often sat on the front porch overlooking their pond, watching nature provide a glorious show.

Just before Greg's aneurysm hit, the couple sat hand in hand on their porch taking in the crisp evening air. The anthem that played like beautiful music in their ears added a new beat that  night when a young mother cat and her two kittens walked hesitantly towards the porch, their wide green eyes begging for some assistance.

Alice called to the cats and felt surprised as they eagerly trotted in her direction. She turned to run inside and grab some meat and a dish of fresh water to offer the feline family; they were clearly in need. The trio of cats were itching their emaciated bodies, covered with fleas and other parasites. The cats purred with delight when they scooped up the meat in their mouths and swallowed, promising nourishment to their ailing bodies. They ate everything that was offered and fervently drank every last drop of water from the dish. Their tails danced with amazement when the bowls were refilled again and again.

Each evening the feline family showed up again to greet Alice and Greg on their front porch. Every night Alice grew more fond of the trio, wondering where they went during the daylight hours. Out of worry for their safety, the couple built a warm covered hut for the cats and placed it on their front porch. They began keeping the food and water dish out for the cats at all hours, hoping they would stick around.

Shortly after the cat's arrival, Greg's heart aneurysm hit and sent him into the hospital. Alice stayed faithfully by his side although Greg was unresponsive and the future was uncertain. Each night Alice drove home so that she could feed the cats, explaining that it gave her a sense of purpose and a point of focus during such a tumultuous time. When Greg went to the hospital, everything seemed so out of control, but coming home each night to the trio of cats felt steady and grounding for Alice.

It was nothing short of a miracle that in his eighties, Greg survived the aneurism. Doctors explained that had he arrived at the hospital even a minute later, the outcome most likely would have been very different. With a lot of intensive care and time, Greg recovered and finally was able to return home to the farm. His recovery was slow and Greg suffered bouts of depression as he wondered if his strength would ever return to "normal". He watched Alice eagerly feed and talk to the cats each night as he too began to grow very fond of the feline trio. The cats became a source of entertainment for the couple, as much as they were a solid anchor in an ever changing routine of life. Greg and Alice found themselves chuckling at the kittens' antics and marveling over the wisdom of the mama cat. Although the couple had always been self-described, "dog people", they were finding in their *Golden Years* that cats had a special place in their hearts too.

In the years since Greg's health scare, Alice has worked hard to provide everything Greg needs in order to maintain his health. She prepares special nutritious meals and is sure to keep his doctor check-ups on schedule. Life has changed for the couple, but all the while the cats have remained a constant source of love and comfort. The cats now run through the hallways of their home and jump onto the couch in the living room at their hearts content. They play with Alice and Greg's dog and they never stop delivering smiles to those wonderful humans that gave them a home. Even on days of particular worry and stress, Alice says that the cats keep her grounded. She has someone to talk to when things get hard and just watching the kittens grow and become healthy and strong has been incredibly rewarding in a multitude of ways. Despite the difficulties life has thrown their way, Greg and Alice keep moving forward, hand in hand, ready for whatever comes their way. The sounds that fill the evening air on their vast farm land encompass their home providing a reassuring, familiar anthem that soothes their souls through the change of seasons; the chirping crickets, the splashing frogs and now the cheerful plodding of little pawed feet rushing through their home.

# Chapter 10: Cat-achino Anyone?

*"Cats are endless opportunities for revelation." –*
*Leslie Kapp*

Imagine grabbing a cappuccino – oh sorry, I mean cat'achino- and lounging in a café with your favorite book, a good friend or heck, just by yourself. You sit back and enjoy your drink while having a loving rescue feline cuddled up in your lap. What could be better? Studies show that pets help reduce depression, lower blood pressure and lessen anxiety. So what's holding you back? Why aren't you out the door and waiting in line? For what, you might be asking? *For the Cat Café of course.*

In April of 2014 the first ever American cat café opened for a limited time in New York City. The café was sponsored by Purina One and the North Shore Animal League. Cat lovers from all walks of life waited outside of the café to grab a chance at this unique experience. Some waited for more than 2 hours to get inside. Once inside, visitors sat on cozy couches and chairs and enjoyed their warms drinks along with the sound of loving purrs echoing from the walls. Sixteen rescues cats trotted throughout the café visiting with guests, and almost every cat was adopted by the end of the temporary cat café.

In 2013 Paris opened a cat café with a dozen resident cats as they promised to offer their guests "purr therapy". While the cats at the Paris café are not adoptable, they are all rescue cats who have found their calling at the cat café providing endless affection and kindness to all who visit. The café's owner shared that guests at the café must follow the rules and be kind and respectful to the cats, but for the cats- they are pretty much free to do as they please. The café reports having record crowds and has become wildly popular in the very populated city.

Other cat cafés have started popping up around the world in the last few years. Montreal, Taiwan, London, Australia, Madrid, Berlin and others are "cat-ching" the excitement. San Francisco is rumored to be opening their own cat café in late 2014 (this would be the first permanent cat café in the United States). Japan is said to have more cat café's than anywhere else in the world at the moment; 150 and counting!

Often those who live in busy cities aren't able to have pets in their apartments, or perhaps they can only have one. Visiting a cat café can furnish benefits that city living may not otherwise provide. What's not to love? A purring cat, adoptable rescue cats meeting new people (potential forever homes!), great coffee and treats and a relaxed environment. What other way would you want to spend your Cat-urday..I mean, Saturday? CNN Travel News writer Ulkrike Lemmin-Woolfrey shared a quote from Lauren Pears, founder of Dinah's Cat Emporium (cat café) in London. "We now have a booking system, because 20,000 people wanted to come into a 30-seat café all at the same time." With numbers like this popping up in cat café's around the globe, the demand is certainly there. Keep your whiskers peeled for a cat café that just might come to a city near you.

# Chapter 11: Cupid's Messenger

*"What greater gift than the love of a cat?" –Charles Dickens*

After more than seventy-years of marriage John and Carol were still as devoted to each other as the day they first met. Over the years they shared their quaint home with their children. Once their children were grown and raised John and Carol welcomed visits from the grandchildren and great grandchildren who came in droves. All the while the couple also shared their home with their favorite breed of dog, the Boston Terrier. Each dog offered his or her loyalty and love to the guardians that had invited them into their ever-changing lives. The devotion of dogs forever warmed their hearts and regardless of the obstacles that inevitably cross each of our paths throughout the journey of life, John and Carol knew that the old saying was true, "A dog is a man's *[and women's]* best friend".

Late into his ninety's John's health began to suffer. On bed rest for more than a year, John most looked forward to visits with his children, grandchildren, great grandchildren and those wonderful four-legged rescue dogs who shared their homes with each of them. John and Carol still resided in the same home where they had lovingly raised eight children; the same home where they taught their children proper manners and the importance of good food. Memories of laughter and echoes of the pitter-patter of feet bounced from the walls of the Cape Cod that together they continued to call home; it's where they made a life and raised a family. But now the home was as it originally began, the two of them alone; a married couple standing side by side and moving through life's journey one moment at a time. When John passed, the house became even quieter. The silence was numbing at first and after a short amount of time that reticence was filled with the sounds of a faint meow.

Following the unfamiliar sound, Carol peaked out the glass of the backdoor to find a cat begging for her attention. She purred when Carol ventured outside to sit down and pet her. She enjoyed the food and treats as well. Each day the cat came back, meowing at the back door like an old friend asking Carol to come outside and play. And each day, Carol greeted the strange cat with a new bowl of food and water and showers of affection. Before she knew it, Carol was letting the cat in and out of her house, upon the cat's request. She named her new friend Kuddles.

Carol made sure Kuddles was neutered and vaccinated and later learned that he lived a few houses down the street. She let her neighbors know that their cat was coming to visit her and they didn't seem to mind. Meanwhile, Kuddles continued popping up at the back door as if on cue each morning, meowing- asking Carol to spend time together. Kuddles sits on Carol's lap and is as gentle as can be. He falls asleep by her side and when he's ready to go he simply trots to the door and gives her a signal. He is a constant source of love and affection for Carol finding his way to her home and her heart just after the passing of her beloved husband. Carol explains, "I still think he [John] sent him when he had to leave."

It was John Bulwer who perhaps said it best, "It's astonishing how little one feels alone when one is loved." His words ring true for Carol as she continues on with life surrounded by visits from her grown children, grandchildren and the familiar sounds of the return of the pitter-patter of feet during frequent visits from her great grandchildren. Her house may feel silent at times as her heart aches for her husband of more than seventy-years, but Kuddles does his best to assist in those very times. It's almost as if Kuddles comes to visit much like a young man courts his future wife; he visits daily bringing gifts of devotion and affection. He sits with her and keeps her company when she is feeling alone. It's as if John sent Kuddles to watch over Carol in his absence; to keep her smiling and to remind her that she is always loved and cared for by the one who won her heart so many decades ago. To some, Kuddles is a cat; to Carol he is cupid's messenger sent from her long time love.

# Chapter 12: Saving Each Other

*"Where there is great love there are always miracles"* –Willa Cather

Her teeth violently gripped the metal cage bars. Saliva ran down the sides of her mouth as she lunged forward in anger. The chunky brown and white Chihuahua had every reason to be angry. After seven wonderful years together, her human guardian had abandoned her in the local kill shelter.

Pure panic embraced the brown and white Chihuahua as the shelter staff reached into her cage with a catch pole – a long metal pole with a rubber loop on the end of it – and pulled it tight around her neck, allowing her to dangle in the air at head height. I couldn't take a breath until her little feet landed safely on the ground. The moment her paws hit the floor and a leash was slipped over her head, her tail began to wag.

Margo wagged her coiled tail and her eyes seemed to gain the glimpse of a spark. We knew we had to save her, what other choice did we have? We didn't know anything about her, other than the fact that the gas chamber had an open door waiting for her if we didn't pay the safety fee and walk out the door with Margo by our side.

Margo sat on my lap with a sense of contentment as she glared out the front window of the car. It seemed as if she was carefully marking each place we passed, as if to tell herself that it was a new beginning; a fresh start. Never again would she know the pain of being locked away in a shelter. Never again would she be next on a list to have her life ended. *Never again.* From this point forward at the rescue, as we promise with every rescue pet, Margo would only know love and compassion. From this point forward Margo would be safe.

The bond between us grew instantly. Margo stuck by my side and I stood by hers. She followed me around as a puppy would. She slept snuggled up next to me at night. She wasn't fond of anyone else, only me and after a period of time this began to concern me. I loved the bond that we had, but I knew if Margo were ever going to have the chance to be adopted into a forever home, she would need to learn to accept others. I began to take her on short drives, on regular walks and she was always present when regular company arrived. She would always throw her small fifteen-pound body in front of my legs when another human approached to say hello. She would snarl and bark; she was protecting me. Having endured a terrifying case of sexual assault and stalking in my personal life, I became concerned that Margo was sensing *my* fear of the world. Was Margo protecting me because she knew I was terrified of being harmed again? Was she simply protecting me the way I had protected her?

It is well documented that animals have a keen sense of energies. If Margo was picking up on my internal struggle to reconnect with the world, *I* had to change.

Although it had been several years since the incident occurred, I had never sought therapy, stubbornly (and naively) feeling that I was *"stronger than needing assistance"*. Margo made me take another look at myself and when doctor's diagnosed me with Generalized Anxiety Disorder, which included frequent panic attacks, I knew it was time to take action. Margo had shown me that in order to take care of her and train her properly, I had to first take care of myself.

I began to talk to a therapist and I discovered the art of yoga. When I would pull my yoga mat out at home, Margo would rush to my side. As I stretched, Margo would lay on her back, all four paws up in the air, staring at the ceiling. As I began to re-embrace loved ones in my own life, Margo began accepting others into hers. Margo's progress encouraged me to continue working on myself. We were going through a journey of discovery together. I was happy to have a partner on my side and I think Margo was too. Margo demonstrated a newfound sense of freedom in her life. She began to play with toys, she ran freely in the yard with other dogs, she greeted guests at the door…she was healing.

The day came when we received an amazing adoption application, nearly six months after her rescue. I admit, my heart sank, but it also fluttered. I had been fostering pets for nearly a decade and yet there was something about Margo that won my heart. We had been through an emotional journey together, we had an unbreakable bond. Was I ready for this? Was Margo?

Laura was everything her application had indicated. She was kind, calm and most of all she was patient. On adoption day, we brought Margo to her new home. Margo hid by my legs, but when Laura bent down with a small piece of chicken, Margo looked at me as if to ask, are you sure this is okay? I nodded as she took a step forward towards Laura's hand. That was the start of their friendship and of my goodbye. Margo trotted after me as I approached the front door to leave that evening. I nearly broke down in tears, but I knew my emotions were being carefully read by Margo and I bent down, gave her a big kiss and told her that she was going to have the happiest of lives here with Laura and that she would forever be in my heart.

I didn't sleep for three nights after Margo's adoption. It was bitter sweet, it always is. You become so attached to your foster pets, yet you want to see them find a forever home surrounded by love. If you didn't reach that goal, it wouldn't be possible to save additional pets in need. Every pet, regardless of age, size or breed deserves a safe, loving and forever home to call their very own.

Nearly a week after her adoption, Laura contacted me with an update. Margo was not only sitting on Laura's lap and following her around the house wagging her tail; she was sleeping with her in bed and loving life. Margo had found exactly what she needed and along the way she helped me begin my own journey of rehabilitation.

Margo's strong spirit remains with me always. We're all on life's journey and life is best lived when we help each other out along the way. Whether or not you remember those who lifted you up when you most needed it, what's important is that you have learned who you are and that you have surrounded yourself with love. Really, is there anything better than that?

*"It's so much better to look back on life and say,*
*'I can't believe I did that'*
*than to look back and say 'I wish I did that."* –Unknown

As published in Chicken Soup for the Soul: "The Dog Did What?" – August 2014

# Chapter 13: Learning What Really Matters

*"Questers of the truth, that's who dogs are; seekers after the invisible scent of another being's authentic core." –Jeffrey Moussaieff Masson*

My life was changing and I didn't even know it yet. While pursuing the next dollar, I had taken a new job thinking that the additional money would provide a lifetime of security and freedom. Years earlier, I co-founded an organization to help animals in need. That was my real passion. Helping animals in need through rescue/adoption and through a multitude of programs such as affordable spay and neuter options; it made me feel alive. From my earliest memory, my two great loves have been helping animals and a fascination of books. Two very different passions, but both were clearly mine. As I tried desperately to stay on the path that I thought was best to follow in pursuit of financial wealth, without realizing it I was losing the two passions I held closest to my heart. My new job increasingly stole more of my time and the stories I had written in my once cherished free time, fell by the way side. The animal welfare organization I co-founded still existed, but I was not sure that I had the time to commit to it as I had once hoped. Instead of growing the organization it was holding steady at best. All of my efforts and energies were given to an office job that I didn't love, in pursuit of the money I feared I needed. It seemed, almost overnight that fear was leading the direction of my life (instead of my passions of writing and helping animals). I was losing myself while chasing the next dollar.

I had a sinking feeling in the pit of my stomach that I forced myself to ignore. But one bitterly cold winter day, between appointments I was heading back to my car when I saw her. She was shivering in the below zero temperatures and my heart sank. I bent down to pet the small, tattered dog and saw icicles hanging from her matted fur. Her paw pads were bloody; her long nails curled painfully under her toes. The small apricot dog allowed me to pet her and spun in several circles with excitement. I placed her under my coat, in an attempt to warm her and walked from house to house in sub-zero temperatures asking if they had seen the dog before or if they knew who she belonged to. Door after door opened with heads shaking back and forth. No one had seen her before, nor did they know where she had come from. Not knowing what else to do, I left my information with each house in the area, in case a guardian should come forward. I placed the shivering dog in my car next to my folders and signs and turned the heat on high. She sat obediently enjoying the warmth of the car's interior, although she seemed nervous at her new and unfamiliar surroundings. I took her home with me that evening and scheduled a veterinary appointment. She was in desperate need of a hair-cut too; her curly fur was matted into her skin. The small dog was covered in fleas (so many that her hair looked gray!) and her stomach was full of parasites and worms. In addition the tattered dog was severely underweight and dehydrated. Instead of working into the wee hours of the night (my usual), I went out to buy dog food for the wiry little dog and spent the evening bathing her. I wanted to let her know that she was safe and the only way I knew how to do that was to clean her up, feed her to her heart's content and spend time with her. Operating the animal rescue, I assumed I would foster her myself and place her up for adoption just as soon as she was healthy enough to be spayed and fully vetted. I didn't have time for a dog in my own life. I was too busy with work (my office job) and I was never home.

But as each day passed, I couldn't wait to get home and see the little dog that had curiously wandered into my busy life. We named her *Lady* and after a few veterinary visits and a nice hair-cut, it was determined that she was a poodle mix. Lady got along well with my cats and she sat on my lap as I worked from home in the evenings (the only time I wasn't working happened to be when I was sleeping- and I was getting very little of that). She curled up at the edge of my feet as I passed away the hours with tired eyes trying to stay focused on work and a head full of endless stress. Lady snuggled up close to my stomach at night when I finally did crawl into bed. In short, she fit right in; even though I reminded myself, I did not have time for a dog. I was pursuing a financial future. Or so I thought. Each day Lady grew healthier and stronger, and our bond also began to grow. She loved to go on walks and really loved to go running with me, which surprised me for a small dog. Without realizing it at the time, Lady's presence was reminding me of my passion for helping animals. Come to think of it, she was reminding me of my passion for other things too; running, writing, relationships (connection). She was reminding me to slow down and actually LIVE life. Lady was teaching me that **when you love your work you are the richest person in the world**. I just didn't realize the lessons she was teaching me yet.

Several months into the job, I was sexually harassed and assaulted at work. It was an unexpected trauma that sent me into quite a shock. After finding the strength to finally leave the job, Lady was there to comfort me through endless nights of nightmares. She was by my side during the  panic attacks that would begin occurring years later. As Lady curled up by my side faithfully every day, she reminded me that there was a higher power at work. When I woke up in pure panic, Lady curled up closer to me; it was her way of letting me know that I was safe and everything would be okay. When I suffered from debilitating panic attacks, Lady would sense the attack and jump into my lap, licking my face and forcing me to come back to the present moment instead of allowing the replay of past events to hold me hostage in my mind. It took five long years before I could gain the strength to seek help in the form of therapy. Once a person full of words, I hadn't been able to find my own voice since the trauma occurred. But Lady didn't force me to talk. She did the best thing anyone could have done for me in that difficult time, she stayed by my side and let me know she was there. Not only that, through my healing she reminded me of my true passions in life. She reminded me with her gentle presence that **life is not about chasing the almighty dollar; it's about**

**chasing your dreams**. It's about living a life full of love and purpose.

The sexual assault occurred just after Lady found her way into my life. On the outside, it may have looked as if I saved *her life*, but I knew that she had really saved mine in every way. The very next year, we grew our animal welfare organization to embrace more volunteers, additional life-saving programs for the community and we officially became a 501(c)3 non-profit organization. I made a commitment to follow my heart. In taking that first step, I was then led back to writing. I began writing articles about animal welfare issues, all the while, Lady stayed by my side.

*My faithful companion.*

Today, our non-profit organization has saved more than 10,000 lives in need and I write for a living. Because one furry life found her way to me just before the moment I needed her most, I have found the courage and strength to live the life of my dreams. The universe works in mysterious ways and I am forever grateful for the signs it provides us, helping us along each of our unique journeys that we so splendidly call *life*.

# Chapter 14: Seniors to Seniors

*"There is no such thing as "just a cat." –Robert A. Heinlein*

After living ten years together with his loving pet guardian, Buddy's human suddenly passed away. Family members didn't want to see Buddy euthanized in a local shelter, and therefore they turned him loose outside of the only home he had ever known, as they moved away. Family members left one last bowl of food and water on the porch for Buddy as they pulled away, never to return again.

A slender domestic short hair black, neutered and front declawed male feline, Buddy had never experienced the great outdoors in his ten years of life and he clung to the front porch, hoping for something to change. Hoping for his food and water bowl to be filled, hoping for a friendly lap to jump into and snuggle…hoping for love. *Hoping to live.*

Several weeks passed and neighbors, concerned for Buddy's well-being, contacted Advocates 4 Animals, requesting help. Having a successful *Seniors to Seniors Adoption program*, Advocates 4 Animals understands that senior pets are not unadoptable, as so often is wrongly believed. Seniors to Seniors adoption programs focus on adopting senior pets to senior humans, making a proper match for both humans and pets. The program matches adopters and pets based on personality traits, lifestyle and comfort level. Matching senior humans with senior pets is a winning situation for both the animals and the humans, as it gives senior pets a great opportunity to be adopted and to experience the greatness of the human-animal bond, living out their days with peace, respect and care. For senior humans, the program offers a wonderful opportunity to adopt an older pet in need and to adopt a pet who is already housetrained and who enjoys a peaceful, calm environment.

Buddy was very lucky to be rescued by Advocates 4 Animals. Upon rescue, he received medical treatment for his dehydration and he was thrilled to have unlimited access to nutritious food. Buddy was taken to an A4Avolunteer foster home in the program, where he had the freedom to move around the home as he pleased. He slept with his foster parents, sat on their laps, ate great food, received wonderful veterinary care and patiently waited to be adopted to a loving, forever home. During Buddy's time in his foster home, Advocates 4 Animals volunteers learned Buddy's personality along with his likes and dislikes. Buddy loved to spend his days lounging in a sunny window and anytime he was invited to curl up on his foster parents lap, he was more than eager to do so. He enjoyed being petted and loved on and he enjoyed being in a calm home environment.

Being ten years old and considered a senior feline, Buddy's foster parents understood that finding a proper adopter for Buddy could take some time. They understood the possibility of never finding a just right home for Buddy and they were committed to fostering Buddy for any length that would be needed; even if that meant for the remainder of Buddy's life.

However, several months after entering Advocates 4 Animals, we received a wonderful adoption application from an individual interested in the Seniors to Seniors adoption program. At age ninety, Martha was a wonderful potential adopter for Buddy. Martha still lived independently in her home. Martha's neighbors were her daughter and her husband, who visited daily with Martha and who agreed to help Martha with Buddy, if the adoption were to take place. Martha's daughter informed Advocates 4 Animals that if Martha should ever have to move into a nursing home facility in the future, Buddy was approved and allowed to go with her; and if anything were to happen to Martha during Buddy's lifetime, Buddy would come to live with her and her husband, without hesitation.

After several conversations, the adoption day was arranged. Both Martha and Buddy couldn't have been happier on adoption day. Buddy immediately went to Martha's lap when she patted him towards her, and the smile on Martha's face was priceless. Martha told Advocates 4 Animals that she had always had a cat or a dog, and she was so lonely without a pet. She promised she would cherish Buddy for everyday of their lives together, a promise Martha kept, as did Buddy. The two quickly became inseparable. Buddy sleeps in bed with Martha, sits at her feet while she eats her meals, and follows her around the house much like a puppy dog. Buddy's tail is always held high and Martha's mouth is always curved up in a smile. Martha's daughter reports that her mother has been more talkative and active since Buddy's arrival. She said, having pets her entire life that she has never witnessed a bond quite like the one between Buddy and Martha.

**Seniors to Seniors** programs can work miracles, for both humans and for pets. Martha and Buddy are living proof of the amazing bonds that can develop between humans and animals, when given the opportunity. Martha and Buddy continue to live out their days with happiness and love for one another and for the world around them. The two, without a doubt, have brought a sense of joy and peace to each other's lives.

As published in Paw Prints- Winter 2010

# Epilogue

*"Our task must be to free ourselves...by widening our circle of compassion to embrace all living creatures and the whole of nature and its beauty." –Albert Einstein*

The first day I transferred to a new college was heart-breaking. Why did I leave my friends? Why did I choose a school that was further from my family? I didn't know anyone on campus and I didn't know how to find the buildings for my classes. The world had just celebrated another New Year holiday and I was sitting alone in a dorm room, surrounded by painted white brick walls and an unknown roommate. What had I done?

I wandered around campus glancing back and forth at my flimsy paper class schedule and the buildings that I passed. I bumped into shoulders, backpacks and kneecaps. Bikes whizzed by me, clipping my heels as my eyes weld up with tears. Glancing at my watch, I realized that I was late to Chemistry class, again. I felt like I couldn't win. Having been an honor roll student my entire life, it felt lonely to be on the outside; to be lost in every way.

As a runner on the schools cross country and track teams, I looked forward to practice each afternoon. It was a chance to be part of a group, to escape the loneliness. It was a chance to be me. Running allowed me to meet others on campus who shared a common interest and it allowed me time to clear my head and begin to ponder what I wanted to do with my life after graduating. The pounding of my footsteps on the city sidewalks gave me a chance to discover myself. I began to think that feeling lost might sometimes be a good thing. If we never feel lost then how would we begin to search for the deeper meaning of life?

Outside of running and studying, life felt empty. When injury struck, I found myself with numbing amounts of free time. I had nothing to do but sit in my small dorm room, wondering what might exist outside of those walls. I wanted to learn more about the city where I was living. I wanted to experience life. My loneliness emerged into a full-fledged curiosity for anything and everything. I began to swim laps in the campus pool, but I still felt trapped. I needed something more. I wanted desperately to discover what life was really about, but I didn't have the slightest clue how to do it.

Having grown up with pets that I had rescued in our family home, I missed having a pet around. When I found the address for the local animal shelter in the phone book, I invited a running teammate to visit the shelter with me. I didn't have a car, so it was essential that I find someone who had access to a vehicle.

"Can you believe this place?" Amy asked in awe. The dark building looked like something from a horror movie, surrounded by a barb-wire fence. A small sign covered in dust hung sideways on the latch of the tall gate.

"It says they're open right now." I shrugged, thinking we must have the wrong place. The building had only one small window and not a shred of green grass. A few minutes later a man emerged from the dark building wearing a red flannel shirt and blue jean overall's.

"What do *ya* need?" He squinted his eyes as if trying to read our minds.

"We were hoping to volunteer, to spend time with the animals…." I stuttered, wanting to run back to the car and drive away quickly.

"Come on in." He muttered as she shuffled towards the door, cigarette pressed tightly between his lips.

Our first day of volunteering led us to the cat room. The cat room was a small 4x10 area with wire crates stacked one on top of the other, filling the entire room from floor to ceiling. Most of the food and water bowls were empty, some filled with dust which told me the cats must have been hungry. Many of the cats were ill, all were starving for attention. They were clearly lonely and they were scared. I could relate and they instantly won my heart. Cats of every age, size and color lined the walls. Their paws reached forward through the rusty steel bars of the cages, begging for help, pleading for attention. They meowed with force, letting us know that they needed help. Amy and I stayed at the shelter until they closed that day. We began going back to the animal shelter every Sunday. We walked the dogs, we provided food and water to every cage, we let cats out of their cages one by one to stretch their legs and feel the sunshine that poured through the tiny window in the next room. We brought pet treats, we made toys and the following year we organized a volunteer day where more than 50 track team members came to walk the dogs and spend time with the lonely pets. Before I knew it, *I* wasn't lonely anymore; I wasn't sitting quietly in a silent dorm room. I was in the city, I was giving back to lives that were in need and I was *living* life. I was learning not only about a great need of our society, but a great need in myself; the need to give back to those who can use a helping hand.

The animal shelter was changing my life as much as we were changing the lives of those we intended to help. Adoptions were increasing, the quality of care had risen by leaps and bounds, the shelter euthanasia rate was dropping and more people were signing up to volunteer. I was ecstatic! I was in awe that one person could really make a difference. I began to learn that we each have the power within us to make miracles happen; it takes three elements: effort, persistence and a positive attitude. With those three qualities, I learned that you can make a difference.

A few short years later, Amy Beatty and I co-founded Advocates 4 Animals, Inc., a 501c3 non-profit animal welfare organization helping to save the lives of death row shelter pets in need. I had turned my loneliness and fear into positive action and change. I had learned to live outside of the confines of the comfortable walls that I once called home. And most of all, I had learned to use what I had already possessed to create something that so desperately needed to exist. Through my desire to discover the world, I co-created a No Kill animal rescue, rehabilitation and adoption group that continues to help thousands of homeless animals annually.

If one person's curiosity can be turned into a life-saving haven for those in need, what else can we accomplish? What else can be done? If we stop living within the brick barriers of our own minds, what we can achieve is limitless; what we can create is inspiring and what we can learn is astounding. If we learn to utilize the gifts we have been given, there is no telling what amazing feats can be accomplished. Feeling lonely and bored are not options, but feeling curious and adventurous, those are not to be ignored.

As published in Chicken Soup for the Soul: From Lemons to Lemonade – Spring 2013

# About Advocates 4 Animals:

*"I wondered why somebody didn't do something.
Then I realized, I am somebody." –Author Unknown*

Advocates 4 Animals is a true labor of love providing life-saving assistance to pets in need since 2003. Through programs such as Rescue/Adoption, Pet Food Pantry, Spay It Forward, Community Cats (Feral Cats TNR program) and Seniors to Seniors, Advocates 4 Animals is making an impact on lives in need. Donating over 10,000 lbs. of pet food to pet guardians in temporary need of assistance *each month*, Advocates 4 Animals strives to help animal's live happy, healthy lives with their humans.

Unlike traditional shelter systems, Advocates 4 Animals houses adoptable pets in home environments as opposed to solitary steel cages typically found at local shelters/pounds. While living in their volunteer foster homes, animals are provided the emotional/social support needed for proper rehabilitation prior to adoption.

One of thousands of happy adopters explained, "Alvin changed my life. I thought I was rescuing a cat in need, especially since adult cats seem to have to wait so long to find adoption. But now I think we rescued each other in so many ways. Alvin makes me smile every day. He brings so much joy and I know he is so grateful for his new life. I wasn't sure at first, but now I know with certainty- Alvin and I are the perfect match. A4A saves the lives of animals in need- but they are also enhancing the lives of so many humans too."

With shelter euthanasia being the number one killer of companion animals in the United States, **we can all take action to make a difference today**. Shelter euthanasia is responsible for more pet deaths than any other disease. In order to eliminate shelter killing and create No-Kill communities around the world, we must understand that no action is too small. Let's continue working together to reform the system and save lives.

**A few ideas that you can do now:**

- Foster-A-Pet in need for your local rescue or shelter organization

- Adopt an adult or special needs rescue pet

- Spay/neuter your pets and encourage others to do the same

- Learn TNR to help feral cats in your area

- Donate funds or requested items to your local animal welfare organization(s)

- Visit your local pound/shelter to socialize with the caged cats and walk the dogs

- Sponsor a pet at your local animal welfare organization

# Save a Life: Donate Today

As a 501(c)3 organization , all donations are tax-deductible. Every dollar donated goes directly to help pets in need. Your support has the power to save another life. Thank you for your kindness! Donations can be made online (*www.Advocates4Animals.com*) or via mail:

**Advocates 4 Animals**
**PO Box 13 Xenia, OH 45385**

You can also join the Advocates 4 Animals Facebook page to witness daily stories of rescue and adoption.
www.Facebook.com/Advocates4Animals

# About the Author

Stacey Ritz is the co-founder and Executive Director of Advocates 4 Animals, Inc. An award-winning writer, Ritz contributes regularly to Cat Fancy Magazine, Dog Living Magazine, American Pet Magazine, *Yahoo!,* Chicken Soup for the Soul books and more. As part of The Op Ed Project's- *Write to Change the World*, Ritz strives to enhance the lives of all living-beings through the power of connection provided through words and stories. *Learn more: www.Advocates4Animals.com* and *www.kittiesinthecity.com.*

**If you enjoyed this book please consider sharing your thoughts with an** *Amazon review.* A portion of the proceeds from book sales benefit animal rescue and adoption efforts.

Made in the USA
San Bernardino, CA
10 December 2018